The Wreck of the
Andrea Gail
Three Days of a Perfect Storm

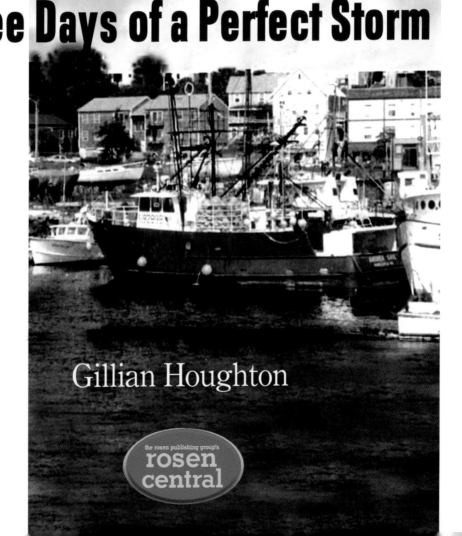

Gillian Houghton

the rosen publishing group's
rosen
central

For Jason

Published in 2003 by The Rosen Publishing Group, Inc.
29 East 21st Street, New York, NY 10010

Library of Congress Cataloging-in-Publication Data

Houghton, Gillian.
The wreck of the *Andrea Gail*: three days of a perfect storm / Gillian Houghton. --
1st ed.
    p. cm. -- (When disaster strikes!)
Summary: Recounts the sinking of the successful swordfishing boat, the *Andrea
Gail*, in what was later called "The Perfect Storm," events leading up to the ship-
wreck, the investigation that followed, and ongoing public interest in the tragedy.
Includes bibliographical references (p.   ).
ISBN 0-8239-3677-5 (lib. bdg.)
1. Shipwrecks--North Atlantic Ocean. 2. *Andrea Gail* (Boat)
[1. *Andrea Gail* (Boat) 2. Shipwrecks.]
I. Title. II. When disaster strikes! (New York, N.Y.)
G525 .H825 2003
910'.9163'45--dc21

                                                                        2001008529

Manufactured in the United States of America

On the cover:
This is the only known photograph of the *Andrea Gail* at sea. It was taken
by Les Nagy/Artsea Photographics, http://www.artseaphotos.com.
On the title page:
The *Andrea Gail* is just visible in a large photo of the harbor at
Gloucester, Massachusetts.

Contents

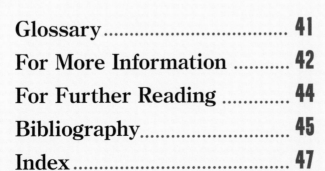

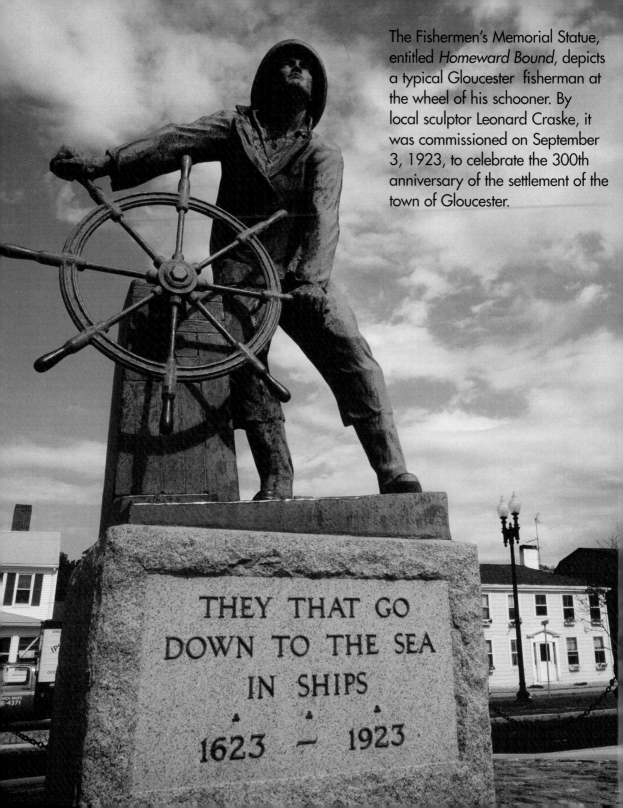

The Fishermen's Memorial Statue, entitled *Homeward Bound*, depicts a typical Gloucester fisherman at the wheel of his schooner. By local sculptor Leonard Craske, it was commissioned on September 3, 1923, to celebrate the 300th anniversary of the settlement of the town of Gloucester.

THEY THAT GO
DOWN TO THE SEA
IN SHIPS

1623 — 1923

Introduction

The *Andrea Gail* steamed out of Gloucester Harbor, Massachusetts, in the early evening of September 23, 1991. The seventy-two-foot-long steel boat was one of the most successful swordfishing boats in the North Atlantic. It began its month-long trip in fair weather with a strong westerly wind pushing it out to the Grand Banks, off the coast of Newfoundland, one of the largest and richest fisheries in the world. After a month of twenty-hour workdays and an especially large haul of swordfish, Captain Billy Tyne declared the trip a success and plotted a course back to Gloucester Harbor. With 40,000 pounds of swordfish packed in ice, the *Andrea Gail* was finally going home.

As the boat approached the warmer waters of the Gulf Stream, however, the wind picked up and the seas swelled. The *Andrea Gail* was heading directly into a once-in-a-century weather disaster, later named the "perfect storm" by a meteorologist who tracked its formation and progress. The Halloween Nor'easter, as it is officially called, destroyed hundreds of New England homes and caused extensive damage to ships of all sizes, from 30-foot private yachts to 100-foot commercial tankers. The *Andrea Gail* disappeared into the towering and cavernous 100-foot waves of the storm. Neither the hulking steel ship nor any of its crew were ever retrieved.

The Rise and Fall of Gloucester

Gloucester was founded in 1623 by a group of English colonists employed by an English trading company, the Dorchester Company of Merchant Adventurers. Finding the harbor teeming with fish, they established a settlement to cash in on the area's natural resources.

The Gloucester fishing industry reached the height of its success in the late nineteenth century. Between 1866 and 1890, annual profits from fishing exceeded $4 million, a huge sum in those days. The harbor teemed with massive schooners and buzzed with the bustle of fishermen mending nets, fitting out boats, and setting out to sea. With this success came danger, however. Each year during the latter half of the nineteenth century, an average of 200 Gloucester fishermen—or 4 percent of the town's population—died at sea. Since 1623, more than 10,000 Gloucester residents have been swallowed by the waves.

Despite the danger, Gloucestermen returned to the sea in greater numbers every year. Over time, the fish population began to dwindle because of over-fishing, and the fishing industry in Gloucester began to decline. By the 1950s, the town's fleet was only about 100 small, independent boats. The harbor's glory days were at an end. Nevertheless, after three decades of bad luck, Gloucester's fishing industry saw unprecedented growth in the 1980s, as more fishermen began to hunt the warrior of the deep—the swordfish.

These workers are weighing and packing halibut in Gloucester during the 1800s.

New Growth in Gloucester

This growth in the swordfishing industry was mainly a result of a shift in fishing techniques. Throughout Gloucester's history, fisher-men hunted swordfish with harpoons, which meant that the fish were caught individually and were usually mature, or adult, fish. Eventually, longlines—thirty-mile-long fishing lines with hundreds of hooks attached to them—slowly replaced the old method of harpooning and greatly increased each boat's catch.

In addition to catching full-grown swordfish, however, longlines also catch pups, or immature swordfish. In the 1960s, the average swordfish harpooned in the North Atlantic weighed 260 pounds. By the 1990s, longliners were catching, on average, 90-pound adolescent swordfish. When the fish are not allowed to mature and reproduce, the population does not replenish itself, and the fishing industry suffers.

In accordance with international fisheries conservation laws, longline boats go farther out to sea each season to fish in international waters in order to avoid overfishing any one particular area. Not only do they have to sail farther every year, they also have to do it faster than ever before. Annual catch quotas—a limit placed on the number of swordfish that can be caught in a year—have pitted boats against each other in a race to catch the most fish before the quota is reached and the order to stop fishing is given. Sometimes these time and distance pressures make boat captains take risks in dangerous weather in order to get a large catch back to shore as quickly as possible.

Billy Tyne: Captain of the *Andrea Gail*

"We took a [heck] of a wave. We went way over on our side. I didn't think we'd make it back up."

**From a radio message to
Captain Charlie Johnson of the *Seneca*.
Quoted in Sebastian Junger's *The Perfect Storm*.**

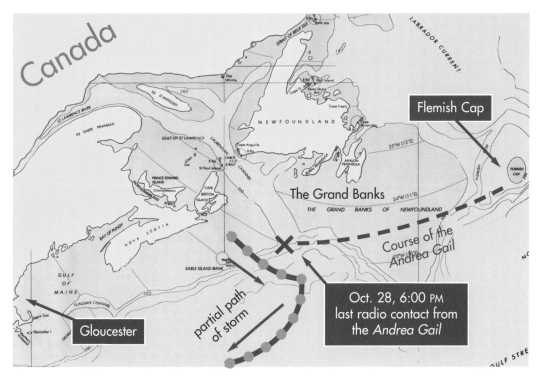

This map of the North Atlantic fishing grounds shows the return route of the *Andrea Gail* and the path the storm was taking when the ship would have encountered it on October 28.

The Race Is On

With the exception of one crew member, the men aboard the *Andrea Gail* were experienced swordfishers. The trip the *Andrea Gail* began on September 23, 1991, would be one of the last trips of the season. It was the captain's and crew's chance to make enough money to pay their debts and survive through the winter. They knew that they had to find fish, wherever they were, and get back to Gloucester as soon as possible. This was a race against the other boats in the swordfishing fleet, and, as they would soon discover, it was an even more challenging, high-stakes battle against nature.

1

The First Days at Sea

As the crew of the *Andrea Gail* set out on their long trip, they enjoyed a brief calm before the storm of activity that would occur once a fishing location was chosen, the long-lines were set, and the enormous fish were hauled in. At this point, they had no idea that they were also enjoying a calm before a far more treacherous storm.

The Boat

The *Andrea Gail* was a midsized diesel boat built in Panama City, Florida, in 1978. In 1987, repairs and structural modifications were made to the *Andrea Gail*. The boat was lengthened by nearly three feet. The port, or lefthand, bulwark was raised three feet, and the whaleback deck (a rounded deck above the main deck) was lengthened by four feet, providing additional protection for the main deck from rain, wind, and waves. These modifications resulted in a change to the boat's center of gravity and stability, and they were not officially registered with the appropriate regulatory agencies. The *Andrea Gail* would ride lower in the water and recover from the roll of waves more slowly as a result of the structural changes.

These photos of the *Andrea Gail* were taken in 1990 by a marine surveyor assessing the boat's condition and value. They were obtained by the United States Coast Guard. They show the main deck *(left)* and the pilothouse *(right)*.

Sunday, October 27

3:15 PM

Having heard the weather forecast and trying to chart the most direct course home, Billy Tyne radios the Canadian Coast Guard to say the *Andrea Gail* is entering Canadian waters.

In addition to six survival suits and a six-person life raft, the *Andrea Gail* was equipped with two VHF radios, a single sideband radio, a fax machine, radar, a weather track satellite receiver, a global positioning system (GPS), a loran (a long-range navigation system), and two emergency position indicating radio beacons (EPIRBs). The radios and fax machine enabled Captain Billy Tyne to keep in touch with the other swordboats fishing the North Atlantic and with onshore meteorological organizations, which send daily faxes regarding weather and sea conditions to all of the boats in the U.S. fleet.

Linda Greenlaw: Captain of the *Hanna Boden*

Greenlaw: "Billy, you seen the chart?"

Tyne: "Yeah, I saw it."

Greenlaw: "What do you think?"

Tyne: "Looks like it's gonna be wicked."

**From a radio message to Billy Tyne.
Quoted in Sebastian Junger's *The Perfect Storm*.**

The radar system and the weather track satellite receiver gave Tyne visual representations of the locations of other boats and of weather systems. The global positioning system tracked the *Andrea Gail*'s own movement using U.S. military satellites, and the loran determined the position of the boat in relation to onshore radio broadcasting stations. Finally, the EPIRBs would broadcast the ship's location, via satellite, to international rescue centers.

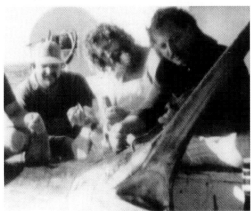

These photos of some of the crew members from the *Andrea Gail*'s fateful final voyage hang on the walls of the Crow's Nest, the Gloucester bar frequented by local fishermen. *Top left*, Bobby Shatford; *top right*, David "Sully" Sullivan; *bottom*, Dale "Murph" Murphy, Michael "Bugsy" Moran, and Billy Tyne.

The Crew

The crew of the *Andrea Gail* gathered at the dock early on the morning of September 23, 1991. The boat's captain, Billy Tyne, and crew member Michael "Bugsy" Moran were both Gloucester natives who had moved to Florida and had made the seasonal journey north by car to secure a site, or place, on board. The other crew members included Alfred Pierre, a Jamaican immigrant living in New York City; Bobby Shatford, a longtime Gloucester native on only his second trip to sea; Dale Murphy, known as Murph, also from Florida; and a twenty-eight-year-old local fisherman named David Sullivan, or Sully to his friends.

Setting Out

After short but anxious good-byes to their loved ones, the crew climbed aboard the *Andrea Gail* and the boat steamed out of the harbor. The 1,200-mile trip to the Grand Banks takes a week, during which time a swordfishing crew catches up on the sleep it will soon be deprived of and prepares the fishing gear.

When the *Andrea Gail* reached the Grand Banks around October 1, Captain Billy Tyne would undoubtedly have scanned the sea for cold-water baitfish—the favorite food of his warm-water prey—and tested the water temperature to find breaks in the ocean currents where the cold and warm waters met. Every captain hopes to find a forty-mile stretch of sea teeming with swordfish.

2

Catching Fish and Heading Home

When an appropriate berth is found—one in which cold and warm water meet, and swordfish encounter plenty of baitfish to eat—the fishing finally begins. The crew's brief period of rest and leisurely preparation comes to a sudden end and is replaced by frantic, exhausting, twenty-four-hour-a-day activity.

Monday, October 28

6:00 PM

Tyne radios the swordboat fleet to report on the weather conditions, saying, "She's coming on strong." This is the last radio contact with the *Andrea Gail*.

Setting the Longline

In longline fishing, a thirty- to forty-mile free-floating mainline is set out each night with more than 900 baited hooks attached. Also attached are hundreds of glowing lightsticks, which, along with the bait, attract the swordfish to the hooks. The line is left in the water overnight, when swordfish follow their meals of cod, bluefish, and mackerel up toward the water's surface. During the night, the boat steams back to the beginning of the line. The next morning, the crew hauls the line, hopefully with a lot of fish attached, back in.

Longline fishing accounts for 98 percent of the swordfish caught in the North Atlantic. Half of the world's total swordfish catch comes from the North Atlantic.

The mainline is spooled around a large drum and protected under the cover of the whaleback deck. Its end is attached to a buoy—a floating marker that shows the crew where in the water the line is located—and fed off the boat into the ocean. As the line unspools, crew members attach leaders (lines that hold a baited hook), floats (to keep the mainline from sinking to too low a depth), and more buoys.

Crew members stand on either side of the mainline at the bait table on the boat's stern and drive the hook through a piece of bait, attach the lightstick, snap the leader to the mainline, and throw the baited end of the leader overboard. After every four miles of line, a highflyer (a float that will show up on the radar screen) is attached. After every eight miles, a beeper buoy radio transmitter is also attached to the mainline. These instruments help the boat to track the mainline's location as it floats upon ocean swells.

After the final buoy is attached, the mainline is cut from the boat. Traveling at six or seven knots, it takes a crew four hours to set thirty miles of gear that cost about $20,000. This is monotonous and dangerous work. The hooks are large and sharp enough to pierce foul-weather gear and skin and pull a man overboard.

The *Andrea Gail's* crew probably continued setting out the mainline late into the evening of their first day of fishing. When they finished, they would have eaten dinner and gone to sleep, while Tyne would have returned to the pilothouse and the ship's radios. The National Oceanic and Atmospheric Administration (NOAA) broadcasts a weather forecast at 11:00 PM each night, after which the North Atlantic captains discuss the day's catch on the VHF radio.

The next morning, the crew would have been on deck by sunrise, ready to haul in the mainline. Using the beeper buoys to determine the line's location, Tyne would have steamed back to the beginning of the mainline at night. The first beeper buoy would then be brought on board and the mainline attached to a large drum and mechanically spooled as the boat went down the line. A part of the starboard (right-hand side) rail would have been removed, and the mainline would run through this gap, making it easier to haul the heavy catches aboard.

Hauling In

The hauler is the crew member who removes the leaders, highflyers, floats, and buoys from the mainline as it is reeled in. Leaders are passed to the coiler, who removes any leftover bait and spools the leader line on a large cart. Leader lines with hooked swordfish are noticeably heavier than bare hooks. When a captain or a hauler feels a certain tension in the mainline during haulback, the crew members ready themselves to bring a swordfish aboard.

Swordfish can live for twenty-five years and weigh up to 1,200 pounds. The average-sized swordfish caught by longline fishers in the North Atlantic weighs 90 pounds. They are worth about $4 a pound to commercial fishers.

The captain slows the boat's engine to an idle to prevent the line from breaking under the weight of the struggling fish. When the leader snap appears above the surface of the water, one crew member grabs it and begins to pull the leader on board hand over hand. A gaffer, brandishing a sixteen-foot-long gaff pole with a sharp hook on one end, stands on either side of the hauler and prepares to thrust the hook into the fish and pull it aboard. Generally, however, the swordfish are still alive as they are being hauled aboard. They often put up a vicious fight that can last for several hours, wildly slashing their swords in every direction and diving deep into the water under the boat. Crew members may cluster around the rail and, when the fish surfaces, stab it with a meathook or a gaff, grab its bill, and pull it aboard.

If the fish is still alive when it is brought on board, the gutter will stab it with a harpoon. All swordfish are decapitated, debilled, and definned immediately, then gutted and placed in the fish hold. Their sharp swords can break through boots and human skin, resulting in a serious injury that almost always leads to infection. Swordfish have even been known to pierce the hulls of boats with their swords.

As soon as this dangerous work of rewinding the mainline is completed, it is time to set out the line again. The crew of the *Andrea Gail* would have enjoyed a brief lunch break after hauling in the mainline before quickly returning to the exhausting work of setting the line all over again.

This work continued day after day for nearly two weeks. The crew worked for nearly twenty hours each day. With each successful haulback, they might have brought from twenty to thirty swordfish on board. On a bad day, they might not have hooked a single fish.

Brewing Storm

As the crew of the *Andrea Gail* set out the mainline for the second straight week, a small storm was growing over New England. It passed over the Massachusetts coast around the middle of October. Some days later, it hit the *Andrea Gail* during haulback. A single rogue wave, thirty feet tall, crashed down on the deck and pitched the small boat on its side. Even with the weight of the catch in the fish hold, which would lower the center of gravity and steady the boat in rough winds, the *Andrea Gail* had difficulty righting itself. It recovered from the roll slowly, Tyne told the other North Atlantic captains over the radio that night. It was late in the season, and the storms were beginning to gain strength over the North Atlantic. This rogue wave was an ominous preview of what was to come.

NOAA meteorologist Bob Case *(inset)* coined the phrase "perfect storm." The storm is visible in this NOAA satellite image. NOAA satellites play a key role in marine forecasting because they help to detect the first stages of storm development. Some 85 percent of forecasters' data comes from satellites.

Billy Tyne: Captain of the *Andrea Gail*

"It's blowin' fifty to eighty [knots] and the seas are thirty feet. It was calm for a while, but now it's startin' to come on pretty good. I'm 130 miles east of Sable."

From a radio message to fisherman Tommy Barrie. Quoted in Sebastian Junger's *The Perfect Storm*.

An Early Return

The *Andrea Gail's* third week at sea was a disappointment; the crew hauled in a slim catch. Tyne decided to steam east toward an area of the North Atlantic called the Flemish Cap, while the rest of the swordfishing fleet was concentrated in an area nearly 600 miles to the south and west. A further annoyance aboard the *Andrea Gail* was a malfunctioning ice machine. Without ice, the catch would begin to go bad and would have to be either thrown out or sold for a reduced price. To compensate for the lost or devalued fish, the boat would have to stay out longer and catch more fish. The longer it stayed out, however, the greater the chance of the catch in the hold getting spoiled. Tyne decided to take the bet that the Flemish Cap would provide him with the huge haul he was seeking.

Tyne saw his luck change around October 18 in the swordfish-rich waters of the Cap. By October 25, the *Andrea Gail*'s fish hold was full. With 40,000 pounds of fish worth upward of $160,000, Tyne turned the boat around and began the journey home. The rest of the fleet remained on the fishing grounds, anticipating at least two more weeks of work. Returning to port early would give the *Andrea Gail* an advantage over the other boats. She would be one of the only boats in dock, creating a small supply of sought-after swordfish. As a result, the market price for each fish would be higher, and each deckhand would earn good money.

The trip home would take about a week, during which time the exhausted crew would catch up on their sleep and would clean and stow the gear. The beeper buoys were disassembled, cleaned, and stowed. As many as 500 floats were returned to the forecastle compartment. Hooks and knives were stored. In the afternoon of October 27, Tyne radioed the Canadian Coast Guard to report that he had entered Canadian fishing grounds and that, in accordance with international law, his gear was stowed. The *Andrea Gail* was nearly a third of the way home.

3

The Storm

As the *Andrea Gail* steamed home on October 27, a cold front pushed east from the Great Lakes to New England. It began as an unremarkable weather system with a small bend, or pocket of low pressure, headed toward the coast of Nova Scotia.

Colliding Fronts

Wind results when air moves from an area of high pressure to an area of low pressure. When fronts of differing pressure, high and low, encounter one another, the wind blows. The greater the difference between the pressure of each front, the stronger the wind. By the time the cold front reached Nova Scotia, it was a raging gale. At the same time, a dying hurricane named Grace began a curve northwest over the Atlantic, while a high-pressure system extended from the Gulf of Mexico northeastward along the Appalachians into Greenland. These three weather systems—relatively harmless by themselves—were on a collision course. Their combined power would be devastating.

The extreme differences in pressure between the low pressure of the Canadian cold front and Hurricane Grace and the high-pressure center streaming in from the south created sustained winds of fifty to sixty knots and wave heights of forty feet. The *Andrea Gail* was about to sail into this tempest, but at this point, there was little to do but keep on course for home. A captain does not always have the time to avoid a storm by heading for harbor.

Battening Down

The crew of the *Andrea Gail* would have undoubtedly prepared the boat as best they could before settling in below decks and waiting for the storm to arrive. They would have stowed loose deck gear in the fish hold, including anything that might clog a scupper and impair the boat's stability. They would have redistributed the weight of deck gear, ice, fish, fuel, and water to balance the hull and improve the boat's ability to right itself in a gale. The fuel and distilled water in their respective tanks would have been transferred to make sure that all of the tanks were as full or as empty as possible. Half-full tanks pose a threat to the stability of the boat because the liquid sloshes around inside, shifting the vessel's center of gravity and enhancing its roll. The crew would also have battened down—or closed tightly—all of the hatches, doors, and portholes with clasps called dogs.

Finally, if possible, the captain would have steered a course away from the Gulf Stream, where the weather is more extreme and the tide current creates unpredictable waves, toward the cold water of the Labrador Current. Cold water is heavier than warm water; therefore, the swells of cold-water waves are generally smaller.

The Calm Before the Storm

Despite the massive storm bearing down on the *Andrea Gail,* the weather throughout the night remained calm. Waves rolled in at about six feet, and the wind blew at about ten knots. By dawn, however, Tyne would have perceived a backing wind, a wind that shifts direction counterclockwise around the compass, suggesting the rotation of a hurricane and indicating bad weather ahead.

An unmanned Canadian weather buoy anchored seventy miles east of Sable Island, records the wave height and wind speed and sends the information to meteorological stations onshore. At 2:00 PM on October 28, its readings showed a sudden jump from calm seas to twelve-foot waves and fifteen-knot winds. Tyne must have known this was only the beginning of the danger ahead. The calm before the storm had come to an end.

Monday, October 28

9:00 PM

As the *Andrea Gail* heads into the edge of the storm, wave heights reach 70 feet and the wind gusts to 90 knots, or 104 miles per hour.

The Battle Begins

The next weather fax to the *Andrea Gail* confirmed the worst fears of its crew. Winds near the center of the storm were predicted to reach speeds of up to eighty knots, and waves were expected to reach heights of up to thirty-five feet. The *Andrea Gail* still steamed through calm water, but the wind continued to shift direction, an ominous indication of the violent weather to the west. Tyne got on the radio and checked in with the rest of the fleet just after 6:00 PM, warning them of the coming storm. He gave his coordinates as 44° north and 56° 4′ west, which was slightly off his original course home. He appeared to be bound for Nova Scotia, which suggests he had decided to weather the storm in the colder, calmer waters of the Labrador Current.

Even with a malfunctioning ice machine and a hold full of perishable fish whose value was decreasing by the hour, Tyne was nervous enough about the oncoming storm to head north, away from Gloucester and the swordfish market. This was the last radio contact with Tyne and the crew of the *Andrea Gail*. Several hundred miles from the closest swordboat, the *Andrea Gail* had begun to battle the waves and the wind as the sun set on October 28.

Linda Greenlaw is a swordfishing boat captain who gained a measure of celebrity when she was featured in Sebastian Junger's book *The Perfect Storm*. She is thought to be the only woman ever to captain a swordfishing boat. After an eighteen-year career of deep-sea fishing, she now lives on Isle au Haut, Maine, where she works her own lobster boat. She has also published two books about fishing.

By 8:00 PM, the *Andrea Gail* would have drawn in range of the phenomenal storm. The barometric pressure continued to drop, creating an even greater divide between the colliding high- and low-pressure systems. The energy created by this divide allowed the storm system to continue to grow and resulted in even stronger winds and higher seas. The height of the waves increased every hour, and by 9:00 PM, the wind gusted at 90 knots, or 104 miles per hour.

Strategies

If Tyne steered the boat downsea (going with rather than against the waves), the square stern would ride up to the top of each wave, instead of cutting through it, as a tapered or rounded stern would do. When a boat is lifted to the crest of the wave, the wave can suddenly break underneath it, dropping the boat into a deep trough of water. The swell that follows such a wave turns the boat to one side or the other, and the captain must use all of his strength to steer the boat straight again. If a boat turns broadside (sideways) to a wave, it could broach, or roll, with the wave. A broached steel boat with a hold full of fish and fuel cannot right itself; it will flood with water and sink.

A boat the size of the _Andrea Gail_ could not have steamed downsea for long; Tyne would eventually have had to turn around and sail head-on into the waves. Probably, he made the decision to do so before the worst of the storm hit. Facing the waves, Tyne would have been able to see each one as it approached, climb its face, and retain more control over the ship as the wave broke on its deck. On the other hand, a boat steaming upsea uses more fuel, and the windows of the pilothouse can be blown out by the weight of a crashing wave.

From the _Andrea Gail's_ pilothouse, Tyne would have had a harrowing view of the storm's massive waves as he struggled to keep the boat upright.

Elizabeth Brannan and Steve Stanford: Coast Guard Petty Officers

Brannan: "As they proceeded toward Gloucester, they would have been hitting the storm, but we can't really speculate on what happened."

Stanford: "We're hoping they might have sensed the storm and turned another way."

From the *Boston Globe*, November 4 and 5, 1991

If he had waited until after 9:00 PM to turn upsea, Tyne would have faced a dangerous maneuver in rapidly worsening conditions. A boat turning upsea is broadside to the waves for nearly thirty seconds, which is plenty of time to become broached when tall, crashing waves are approaching every eight or nine seconds. At this point, all thoughts of getting their fish to port would have been forgotten. The crew of the *Andrea Gail* was in a desperate struggle just to survive.

Sailing Blind

As the night wore on, Tyne's muscles must have ached trying to control what was essentially a rudderless boat on a roller coaster of gray water. As he climbed the face of each wave, or crashed straight through it, the wind could have appeared from any direction and lashed the bow of the boat to either side. When another boat in the fleet, the *Allison*, tried to radio Tyne around 11:00 PM, there was no response. It is possible that the *Andrea Gail*'s antennas were broken or blown off by the wind, which would mean the boat's GPS, radio, weather fax, and loran would no longer work. Without the GPS and loran, Tyne could not have reliably determined his location or the locations of other boats. Without a radio, Tyne could not make contact with the rest of the swordboat fleet or with maritime authorities and rescue teams. Without a weather fax, the crew would have had no way of knowing what else the storm had in store for them.

It is also possible that the power of the wind and the water had blown out the half-inch-thick windows in the pilothouse by the late evening of October 28. To repair them, members of the crew—with rope tied around their waists and secured on board—would have had to leave the safety of the forecastle, climb onto the whaleback deck, and drill sheets of plywood into the now-empty window casements. Meanwhile, the pilothouse would have been filling with water and shrieking with wind. With plywood for windows, the view from the pilothouse would have been partially or completely obscured. Manning the helm, Tyne would not have been able to see what was coming next.

4

The Wreck

The *Andrea Gail,* out of all radio and radar contact, was only a tiny speck in the vast ocean. The night was just beginning. The massive storm showed no sign of letting up, and Billy Tyne must have wondered if he and his crew would live to see the sunrise.

The Eye of the Storm

The wind and waves calmed briefly around midnight, but by 1:00 AM on October 29, the *Andrea Gail* was passing through the eye of the storm. A meteorological buoy south of Sable Island recorded peak wave heights of 100 feet, the equivalent of a ten-story building, for several hours on the afternoon of October 29. The size of the waves prevented the buoy from accurately measuring the wind speed, which has since been estimated at around 120 miles per hour. The storm did not let up for the rest of the day. By the evening of October 29, boats twice the size of the *Andrea Gail* were awash in water.

Throughout this stormy day, Tyne did not radio the U.S. Coast Guard or trigger his EPIRB (which would have sent out a distress signal). He might have been optimistic about the *Andrea Gail*'s chances up until the very end, or he might have thought that a rescue was impossible under these conditions. The *Andrea Gail* was hundreds of miles from land; it would have taken the closest rescue vessel, the Canadian Coast Guard cutter *Edward Cornwallis*, thirty-six hours to reach it. The Coast Guard would have called on all other nearby seagoing vessels to sail toward the *Andrea Gail*, but once they arrived, there would be little they could have done to rescue the men or the boat. It would have taken a helicopter rescue unit over three hours to reach the boat, and if they arrived at night, a rescue would be very difficult. Tyne could have readied the life raft if the boat capsized and began to flood, but the six-man raft would not have withstood the high seas any better than had the steel swordboat. The crew's only course of action was to keep the boat running as smoothly as possible under the circumstances and hope that they would get lucky.

How the End May Have Come

At any moment, Tyne must have expected a single wave to wreck the *Andrea Gail*, but he may have been uncertain about exactly how the boat would be destroyed. If a boat is headed upsea, it has to climb the face of each wave. If it cannot power itself to the top and instead slides back down the face of the wave, the stern can sink into the trough while the bow is caught by the crashing crest of the wave. The boat is then flipped backward and upside down. This is called pitchpoling. The overturned boat remains afloat for some time, buoyed by the air trapped in the hull, giving the crew a chance to escape. However, it does not have the ability to right itself.

Similarly, a boat can founder. This occurs when the boat, caught near the trough or on the face of a wave, is driven straight underwater by the power of the breaking wave. The weight of the water would make the windows implode and the dogs pop open. The bilge pumps would be overwhelmed or entirely useless if the power shorted out. As a result, the boat would flood with water and sink almost immediately, not giving the crew a chance to escape.

The *Andrea Gail* seems destined to pitchpole under the weight of this gigantic wave in this still from the movie *The Perfect Storm*.

Tuesday, October 29

1:00 AM

The *Andrea Gail* enters the eye of the storm. Tyne had probably decided to head upsea, against the crashing walls of water, which destroyed the boat and its crew.

A third way in which a boat can be destroyed during a storm is if it turns broadside to a wave, broaches, and begins to take on water quickly. The crew then becomes trapped in the boat or are sucked under water by the vacuum created as the boat sinks.

The point at which a boat can no longer return to an even keel is called the zero moment. Although we have no way of knowing exactly how the *Andrea Gail* met its fate, the boat must have reached the zero moment quickly, within minutes, because nobody had the chance to arm the EPIRB. A towering wave may have appeared—as if out of nowhere—perhaps blocking out the sky.

The sound of the wave breaking must have been deafening and the utter despair onboard the *Andrea Gail* palpable. In an instant, the boat would have been sinking quickly into the dark, gray-green water that was flooding the hold. The sudden darkness might have been fitfully illuminated by sparks as the electrical equipment shorted out. The crew's last few moments must have been a blind chaos of tumbling gear, confused and panicked attempts to make sense of the upside-down passageways, and a relentless onslaught of cold, dark water.

The Search

On the morning of October 29, the *Andrea Gail*'s owner, Bob Brown, frantically radioed his boat and received no answer. By the evening of October 30, Brown alerted the U.S. Coast Guard of the boat's disappearance, and, later that night, he contacted the Canadian Coast Guard. Rescue authorities and other boats in the swordboat fleet tried and failed to contact the *Andrea Gail* on every radio frequency. The U.S. Coast Guard called every town and hamlet along the northeast coast to see whether the *Andrea Gail* had drifted into harbor; once again, their efforts met with no success.

During the storm, U.S. Coast Guard swimmer Chief Petty Officer David Moore *(left)* and hoist operator Petty Officer Scott Vriesman, aboard a Coast Guard helicopter, prepare to rescue three stranded sailors and three Coast Guard crew members who had come to their aid. The Coast Guard swimmers jumped out of the helicopter into the North Atlantic's teeming waters to pull all six to safety.

Fifteen rescue planes were deployed and began crisscrossing the North Atlantic in search of the boat. Over the next ten days, they covered an area of 116,000 square miles but saw no sign of either the battered vessel or its crew. Then, on November 1, a fellow swordboat captain on his way home in the wake of the storm saw a cluster of fuel drums floating in the water 100 miles south of Sable Island. Each barrel had the letters *AG* stenciled on its side. The U.S. Coast Guard was notified of this discovery, and the search area was expanded. Though the drums did not necessarily indicate that the ship had sunk, their discovery was not a promising sign.

On November 4, a propane tank and a radio beacon, both labeled *Andrea Gail*, were found washed up on the shores of Sable Island. The beacon, part of the mainline fishing gear, was turned on, which may indicate an attempt by Tyne to connect the boat with onshore authorities using their only functioning electronic equipment. On November 5, an EPIRB, identified by its serial number as belonging to the *Andrea Gail*, was found on Sable Island. It was turned off, meaning that for one reason or another, crew members were not able to use it to send a distress signal.

Investigations and Improvements

Late in the evening of November 8, rescue workers gave up the search for the *Andrea Gail*. Following an investigation into the ship's disappearance, recommendations were made to impose

Robert Brown: Owner of the *Andrea Gail*

"[The *Andrea Gail* and its crew] were officially reported overdue on Nov. 1st. I told [the Coast Guard] I was afraid the boat was in trouble and I feared the worst . . . We have hope that the boat is o.k. and that it's just lost its communication . . . I hope they continue searching for a couple more days."

From the *Gloucester Daily Times*, November 5, 1991

stricter stability tests on commercial fishing boats and to regulate the documentation of alterations made to them. If these procedures had been in place in 1991, questions may have arisen over the *Andrea Gail*'s stability following its modifications, and a careful inspection might have helped to ensure its seaworthiness in stormy weather.

In the years following the wreck of the *Andrea Gail*, the technology necessary to provide more accurate and long-range weather forecasts has improved. The Advanced Weather Interactive Processing System (AWIPS) allows weather forecasters to analyze many kinds of data more efficiently and detect weather patterns more quickly nationwide. This enables the National Weather Service (NWS) to send out severe weather watches faster, reducing the risk of disaster on land and at sea. If this technology had existed in 1991, the *Andrea Gail* might have had the time to sail away from the storm and out of harm's way.

After the search was called off and the funeral services were held, the financial dependents of several of the *Andrea Gail*'s crew members initiated lawsuits against the boat's owner, Robert Brown.

Conclusion

The case was settled out of court. Though the boat's undocumented modifications raised doubts, it would have been difficult to prove in court that the *Andrea Gail* was less than seaworthy.

By most accounts, the *Andrea Gail* was a trim and sturdy ship, even after its alterations. Its owner was known to be precise and careful, and the boat was well maintained. In the end, however, these precautions held little sway in the face of nature. The changes that resulted from the recommendations made in response to the *Andrea Gail* investigation may prove equally futile when an otherwise seaworthy and expertly captained ship confronts a storm of the magnitude of the Halloween Nor'easter. Even the most carefully engineered boat would be put to a severe test in towering, ten-story waves and winds that whip the cables on deck into a frenzy. The ocean is essentially a wild thing, even when calm. Its sudden shifts and ferocious waters should never be treated lightly. An unsinkable boat will never be built. Sailors will forever go to sea only at their own peril.

In 1997, journalist Sebastian Junger published an account of the *Andrea Gail's* disappearance entitled *The Perfect Storm*, which became a best-selling book and inspired a movie of the same name. Curious tourists began to

People attend a memorial service for lost fishermen at St. Ann's Church in Gloucester. Residents of Gloucester are used to mourning, as some 10,000 local sailors have disappeared at sea since the 1620s.

Angela Sanfilippo, president of the Gloucester Fishermen's Wives Association *(left)* hugs fellow member Nina Groppo during the dedication of the Gloucester Fishermen's Wives Memorial in Gloucester on August, 5, 2001. Since 1623, more than 10,000 fishermen from Gloucester have been lost at sea.

arrive in Gloucester in droves, eager to visit the swordfishers' favorite bars and take pictures of the battered boats in the dilapidated harbor. The popularity of the book and movie suggests their audiences' fascination with the unpredictable power of the ocean. Like the earliest Gloucester residents, who were alternately fearful and entranced by what lay beyond the shallows, we are still eager to enter into the maritime world of the swordfishers, if only through our imaginations.

Glossary

bow   The front portion of a boat.

broadside   With the side of the boat facing a wave or wind.

downsea   Heading in the same direction as the wind and waves.

forecastle   A small raised deck toward the bow of the boat that houses the crew's quarters.

founder   To be driven straight underwater, flood, and sink.

front   The boundary between two air masses that differ in pressure.

knot   Measurement of speed in nautical terms; one knot equals one nautical mile per hour.

pilothouse   The room at the top of the forecastle where the navigation and communication controls are kept.

pitchpoling   When the stern of a boat is caught in the wave's trough while the bow is caught by the wave's breaking crest. The boat is flipped end over end, floods, and sinks.

schooner   A three-masted sailboat used for commercial and military purposes in the nineteenth century.

scupper   A hole at the base of a gunwale that drains water and fish guts from the floor of the main deck.

trough   The bottom or valley of a wave.

upsea   Heading into the wind and waves.

whaleback deck   The above-deck constructions, including the forecastle and pilothouse, at the bow of the boat.

zero moment   The moment after which a boat cannot right itself and regain an even keel.

For
More
Information

Organizations

Cape Ann Historical Association and Museum
27 Pleasant Street
Gloucester, MA 01930
(978) 283-0455
Web site: http://www.cape-ann.com/historical-museum

National Marine Fisheries Service
1315 East-West Highway, SSMC3
Silver Spring, MD 20910
Web site: http://www.nmfs.noaa.gov

National Ocean Service
1305 East-West Highway, SSMC4
13th floor
Silver Spring, MD 20910
(301) 713-3070
Web site: http://www.nos.noaa.gov

National Weather Service
1325 East-West Highway, W/OS
Silver Spring, MD 20910
(301) 713-0090
Web site: http://www.nws.noaa.gov

U.S. Coast Guard Headquarters
2100 Second Street SW
Washington, DC 20593-0001
(202) 267-1587
Web site: http://www.uscg.mil

Web Sites

Due to the changing nature of Internet links, the Rosen Publishing Group, Inc., has developed an online list of Web sites related to the subject of this book. This site is updated regularly. Please use this link to access the list:

http://www.rosenlinks.com/wds/wrag/

For Further Reading

Garland, Joseph E. *Down to the Sea: The Fishing Schooners of Gloucester*. Boston, MA: David R. Godine, Inc., 2000.

Garland, Joseph E. *Lone Voyager: The Extraordinary Adventures of Howard Blackburn, Hero Fisherman of Gloucester*. New York: Simon and Schuster, 2000.

Greenlaw, Linda. *The Hungry Ocean: A Swordboat Captain's Journey*. New York: Hyperion, 2000.

Junger, Sebastian. *The Perfect Storm: A True Story of Men Against the Sea*. New York: Harper Perennial, 1999.

Monahan, Dave, ed. *World Atlas of the Oceans: More than 200 Maps and Charts of the Ocean Floor*. Willowdale, Ontario: Firefly Books, 2001.

Perley, Sidney. *Historic Storms of New England*. Beverly, MA: Commonwealth Editions, 2001.

Reynolds, Josh. *The Port of Gloucester*. Beverly, MA: Commonwealth Editions, 2000.

Bibliography

Bourne, Russell. *The View from Front Street: Travels Through New England's Historic Fishing Communities*. New York: W.W. Norton and Co., 1989.

Chow, Cheong. "Coast Guard Continues Search for Missing Gloucester Vessel." *Boston Globe*, November 5, 1991.

"Coast Guard Calls Off Search for Boat from Marblehead." *Boston Globe*, November 10, 1991.

"Coast Guard Searches for Boat." *Boston Globe*, November 4, 1991.

Garland, Joseph E. *Down to the Sea: The Fishing Schooners of Gloucester*. Boston, MA: David R. Godine Inc., 2000.

The *Gloucester Daily Times* Perfect Storm Page: http://www.ecnnews.com/storm/stormhom.htm

Greenlaw, Linda. *The Hungry Ocean: A Swordboat Captain's Journey*. New York: Hyperion, 2000.

Junger, Sebastian. *The Perfect Storm*. New York: Harper Perennial, 1997.

Longino, Bob. " 'Perfect' Fishing Town Girds for Storm of Tourists." *San Diego Union-Tribune*, July 8, 2000.

Safina, Carl. "Imperfect Fishing Doomed Crew." *Newsday*, August 10, 2000.

Sallah, Michael D. "Old Fishing Town Rides Out Storms."
    Pittsburgh Post-Gazette, July 16, 2000.
Sullivan, Jack. "Gear Missing from Boat Found on Canadian Isle."
    Boston Globe, November 7, 1991.

Index

About the Author

Gillian Houghton is an editor and freelance writer living in New York City. She is an experienced sailor but an unsuccessful fisher who has long been intrigued by the mystery and power of the ocean.

Photo Credits

Cover © Les Nagy/Artsea Photographics; pp. 1, 13 courtesy of the Crow's Nest; pp. 4–5 © Jim Zuckerman/Corbis; p. 7 © Culver Pictures; p. 9 © the Defense Mapping Agency Hydrophotographic/Topographic Center; pp. 11, 16, 28 © U.S. Coast Guard/United states Department of Transportation; p. 18 © Index Stock; p. 20 © NOAA; pp. 27, 39, 40 © AP/Wide World Photos; p. 33 © The Everett Collection; p. 35 © Petty Officer Doug Ayres/USCG.

Series Design and Layout

Les Kanturek